# Glory Girls:
# Pon Di Road!

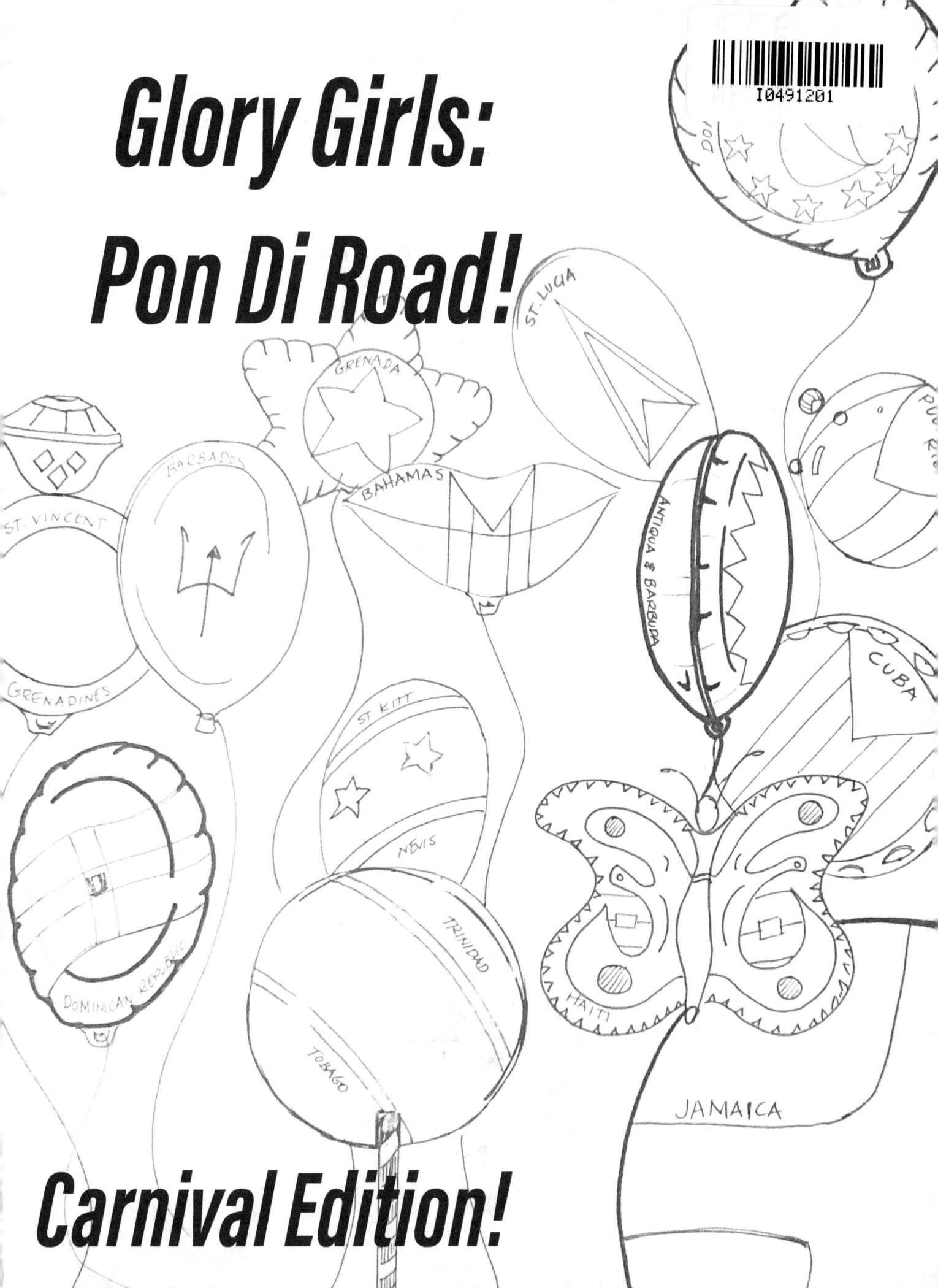

# Carnival Edition!

ISBN:
First Edition: October 7th, 2023
Cover photography by Nicole Elaine Avery. 2023
Interior artwork by Nicole Elaine Avery. 2023
Canva is the site source for puzzles.

BE Publishing
A division of Broadway Empire, LLC
Broadway Empire is a media company.
Printed in the United States of America

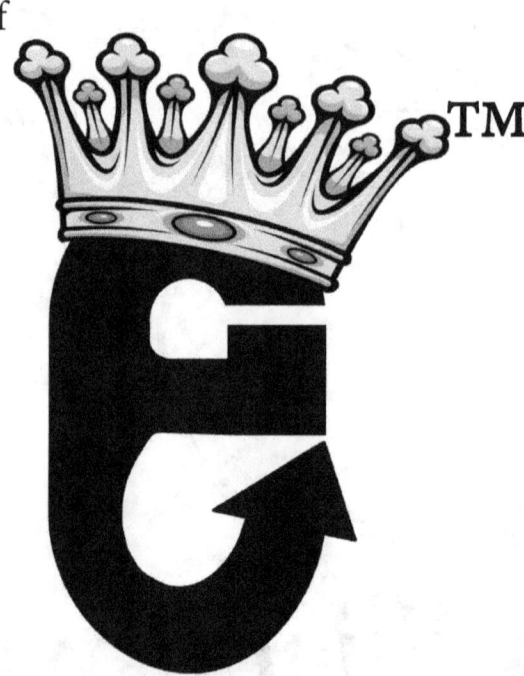

# The Glory Girls™ take the West Indies by storm! They play mas* on fourteen (14) Caribbean islands.

*Like many dances created by captive Black peoples, Mas began as a mimicry of the way White Plantation owners moved. Learn more about each nation/territory through activities found on the even pages. Have your tablet handy, or interview your Ca-ribbean friends and family, for clues.** There are scenes to color on the opposite pages. This book is intended for the use of girls in third through fifth grade, although ANYONE can participate. Faces have been left blank for the user's interpretation. That means you have an opportunity to make anyone of the GLORY GIRLS™ look just like you! Have fun!! (For answers to activity puzzles, and mazes, refer to the end of the book.)

# Antiqua & Barbuda

1. _____ is Antiqua & Barbuda's national dish.

2. Antiqua & Barbuda are a total of _____ islands.

3. An alternate name for Antiqua & Barbuda is _____.

4. Green _____ can be found visiting guests on their morning walks.

5. This mountain has the same name as the 44th US president. What mountain is it? _____.

## RIDDLE

I start with the letter C, my cousins are professional high jumpers, and I can be found on a green field in Antiqua. What am I ?

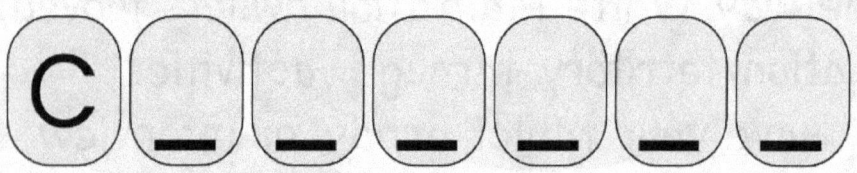

Solve the riddle bu placing the correct letters in the lanks.

### TIC-TAC-TOE

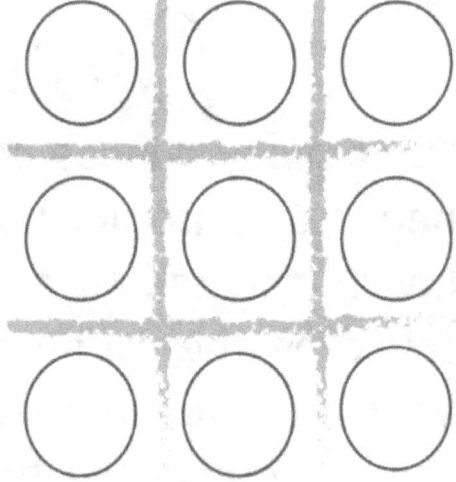

How many words can you make from the proper nouns ANTIQUA and BARBUDA? (No, you can't use the word "and.") Write your answers, below...

_____ _____ _____ _____ _____ _____

_____ _____ _____ _____ _____ _____

_____ _____ _____ _____ _____ _____

_____ _____ _____ _____ _____ _____

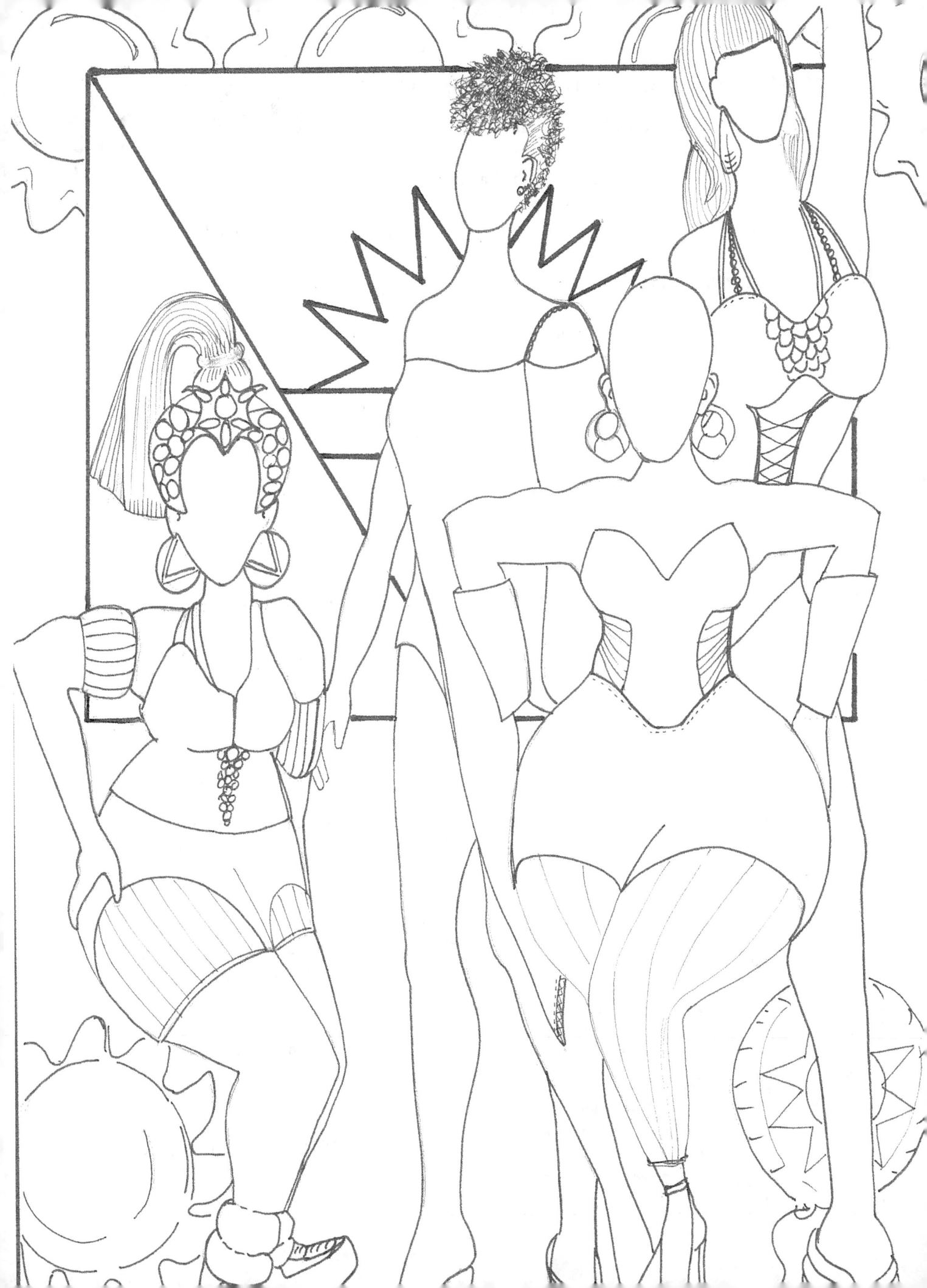

CAN YOU FILL IN THE BLANKS WITH THE CORRECT WORD?

# Bahamas

1. What U.S territory sits next-door to the Bahamas? _____

2. There are more than _____ islands in the Bahamas.

3. Before claiming to discover the Bahamas, Christopher Columbus allegedly discovered _____.

4. _____ is another name for the Bahamas.

5. What four legged animal can be found swimming in the Bahamas? (Not a dog or cat. Try again.) _____

6. _____ is a famous movie fillmed in the Bahamas.

7. Unlike other beaches, Bahamas has _____ colored sand.

8. There is an _____ park in the Grand Bahamas.

9. The ocean water in the Bahamas is clear due to the _____ depth.

10. Pittsburgh major league baseball, Peter Pan, and the Bahamas all have _____ in common!

```
q v m j z s f h e n r h w s h k e b v z v o c o u
i v l g d g u l m p s l n l m j o r i x d y l c j
l s w q n p e f c o d i l c j j v v s m h s o a x
b j m k e u f a h k l u w m x m i s k z i q w b f
o c q t t w t p d k e r x k d r c l p p w n b a p
i z t h h i z k c t j p k s z w a n d r o s i y w
q c e v s m q a x m z o g j i s a i h q a l n b k
p r g l k h z o h v a d k s m k k f r s z f d q v
a t a n p d v v z w w y v k t s j a o f u g a e g
k n u n s k v l k c k z a h r l c v d j p w k z g
d b x i h c g f u p s m z g d c i e a g m t l x m
d w j m j x f h m f t s s b u e j e v e m f d d c
v e a n v u p w d s f p w e a a y c l e f u q c d
q g g y r o a v l s x j a d r p m n w a v o b s z t
h n d z w c p u c l z n l r i b a a s r e v x u b
f k u j e q i z u e a i n y v j o h n p a i h y p
s f m k c w d m c l w s s i x d u e a o x u j v v
o a s v e g t s s n t h b s b c m x s b z s i h k
j b s x g t o i c z t w f l p s q w f u d f k c i
v i m m b m g y a b e e r a k w p o g a s n f o d
l x i g w n q a e s m l f n x v b p g m c o a e d
a j n w o c r q v c d l h d x u g k s w s r q r h
z a w l y j a f k o h s o s r y l h s d t r m t g
h a r b o u r n v k e s p h y i e b w c r s j s i
d n a l s i d e k o o r c t c m f a i e n q j s e
```

# WORD SEARCH

Can you locate the words listed at the bottom of the page in the group of letters to the left?

| | | |
|---|---|---|
| Abaco | Eleuthera | Harbour |
| Acklins | Crooked Island | Mayaguana |
| Andros | Grand Bahama | Spanish Wells |
| Bimini | San Salvador | Cat Islands |

Berry Islands   Long Island

Cirlce each word.

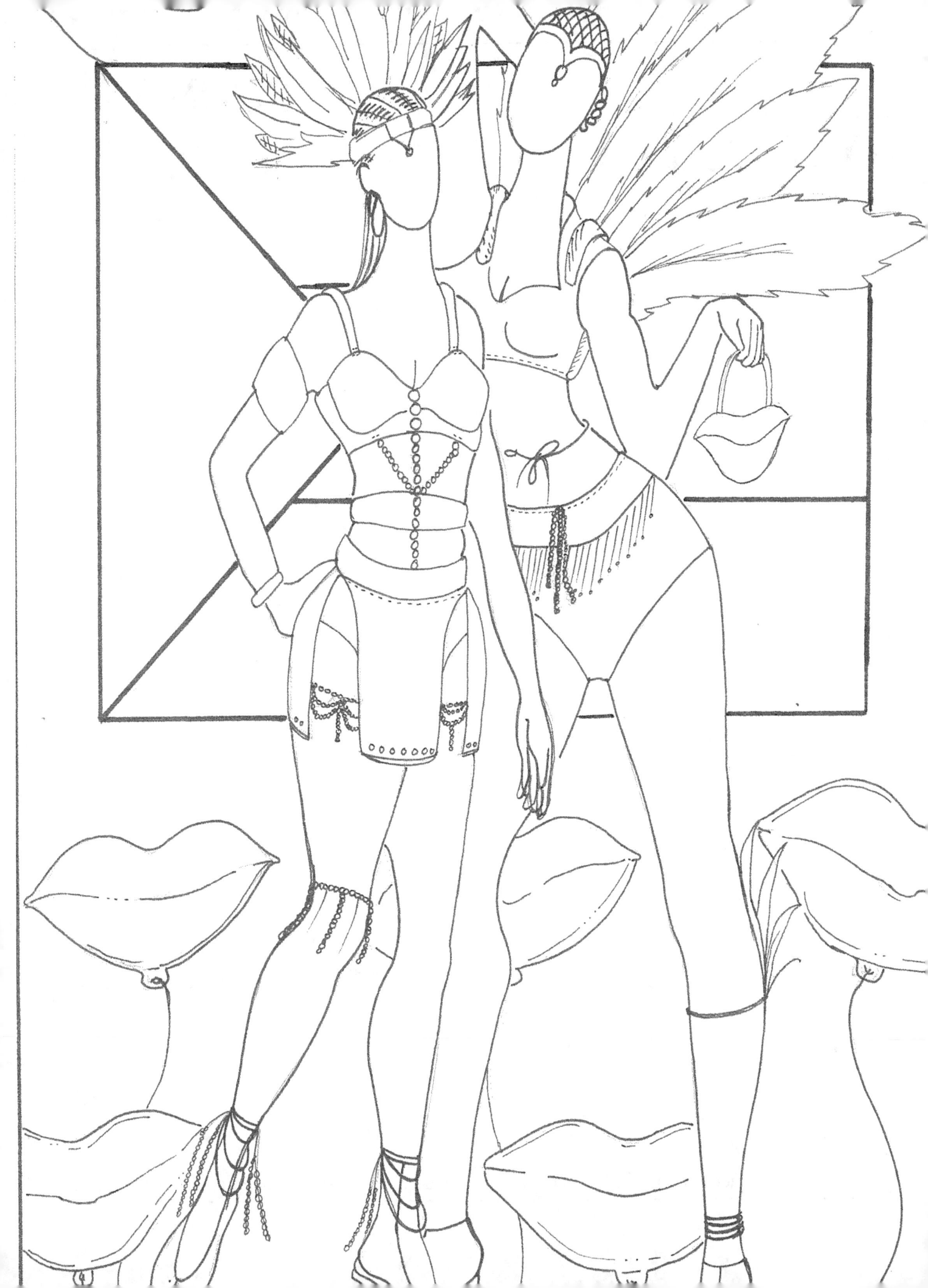

# Barbados

2018 The first female Prime Minister was elected

Barbados is the home
of R&B singer, and
super-star, *Rhianna*.

In Portugese, Barbados means "the bearded ones." The island was named after their popular bearded fig trees.

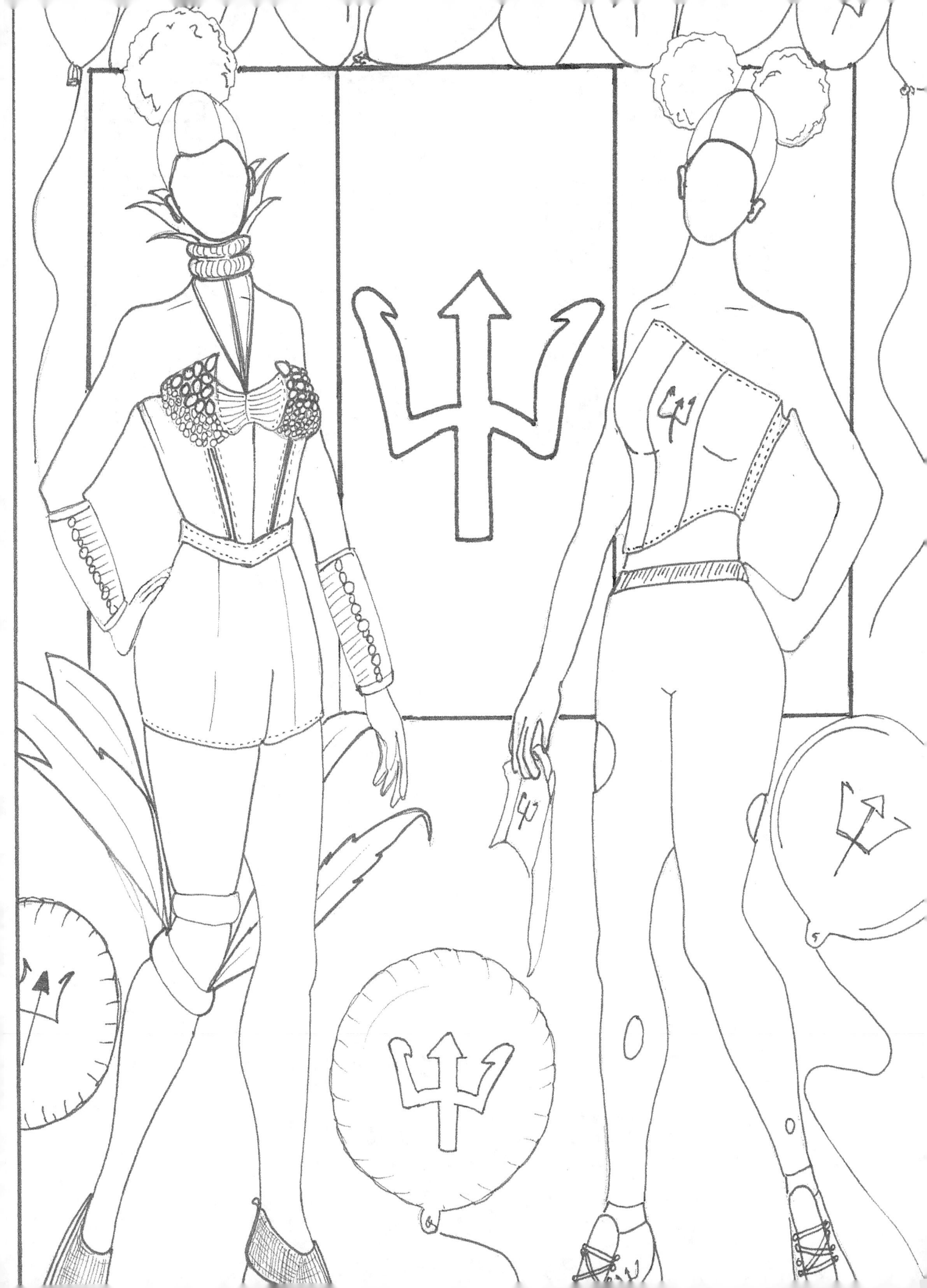

# Cuba

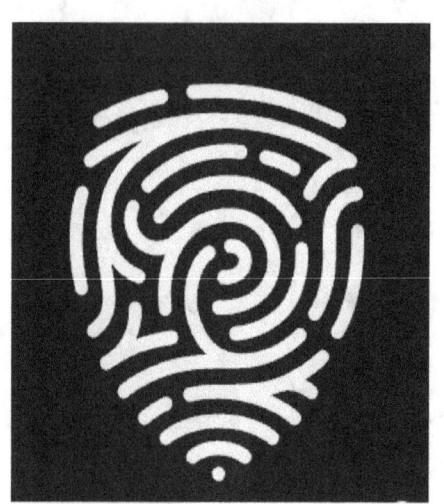

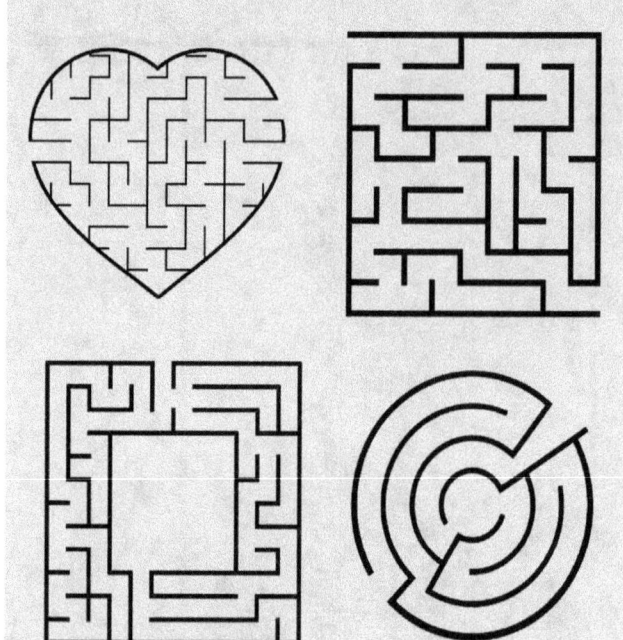

A

ACROSS

1. The Cuban flag is similar to _____'s.

C

DOWN

2. US Dollars have been _____ in Cuba.

3. Cubans love to play _____ as much as they do baseball.

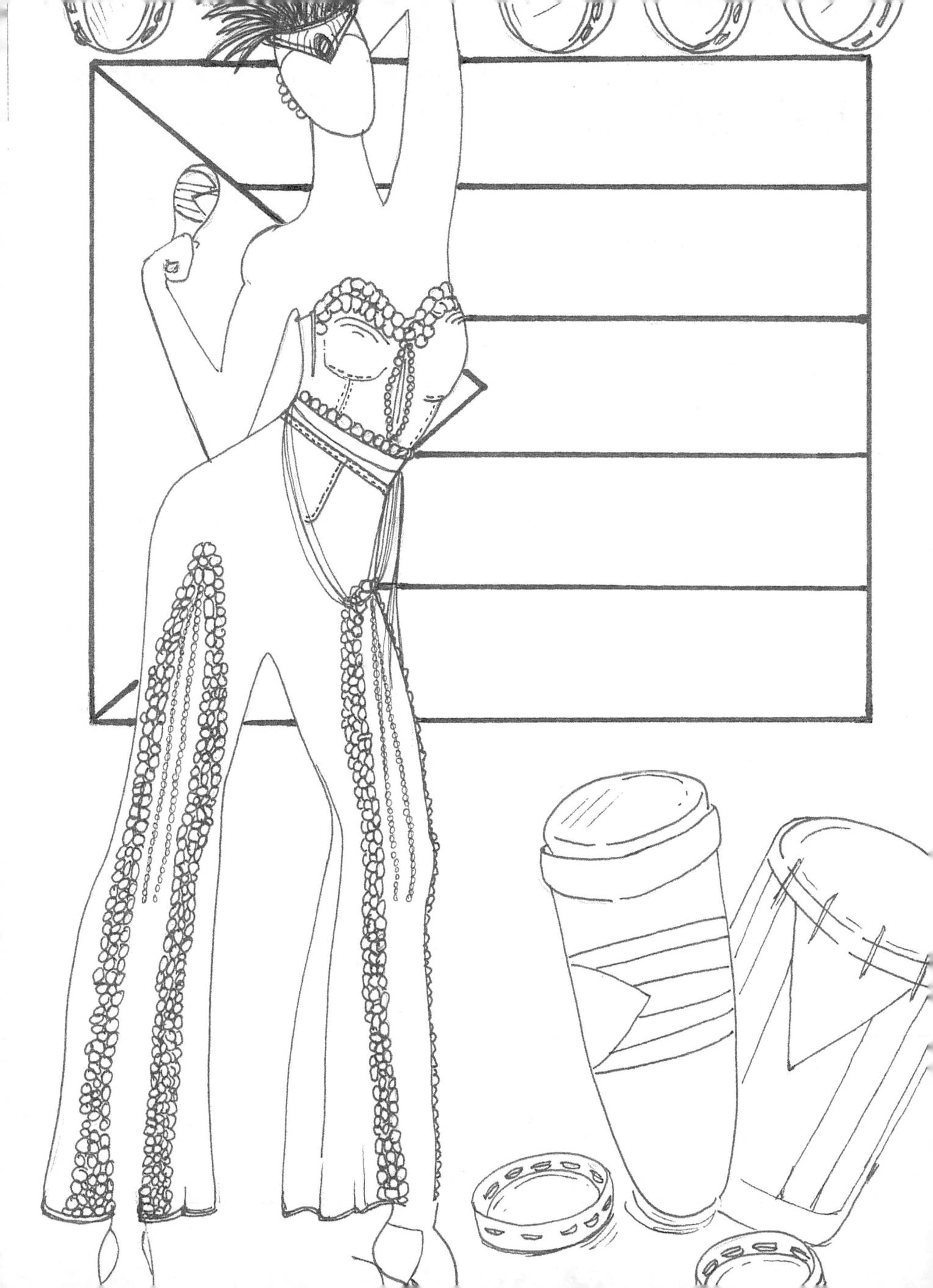

# Dominica

Can you solve the secret message using the key below?

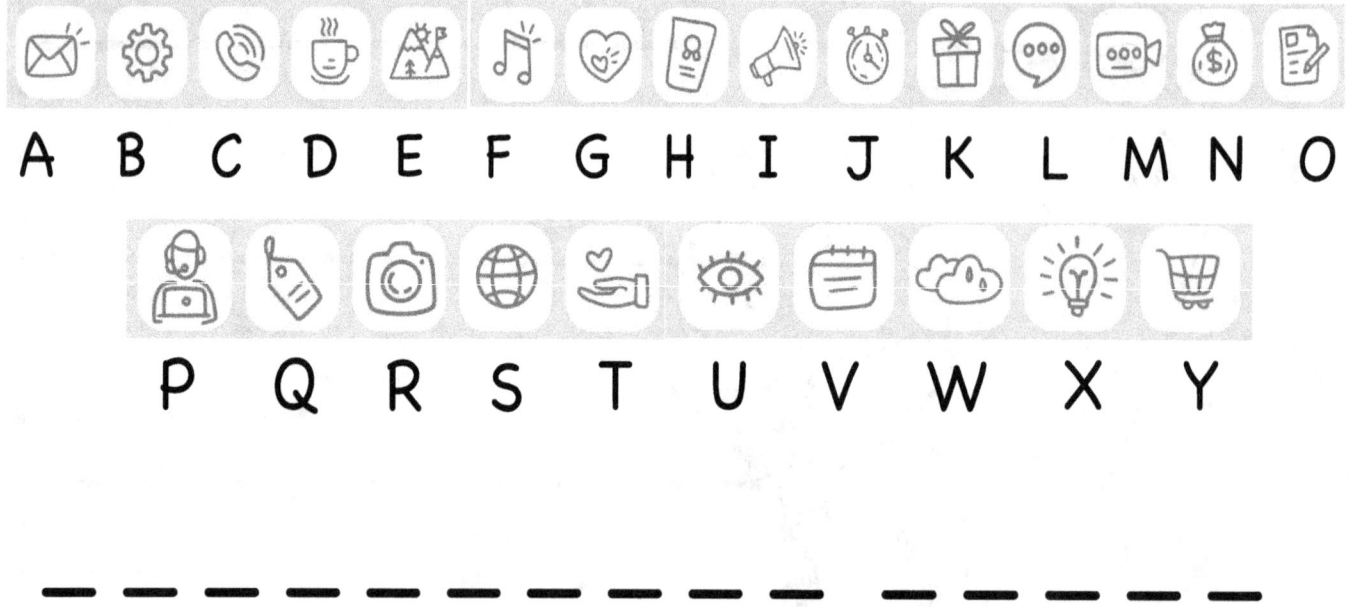

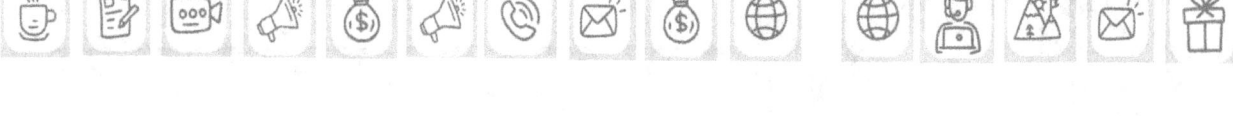

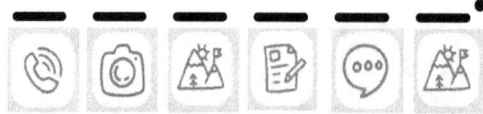

FIND A FUN FACT ABOUT DOMINICA AND CREATE YOUR OWN MESSSAGE FOR A FRIEND TO SOLVE. HAVE FUN! (You will have to create your own symbol for the letter "Z.")

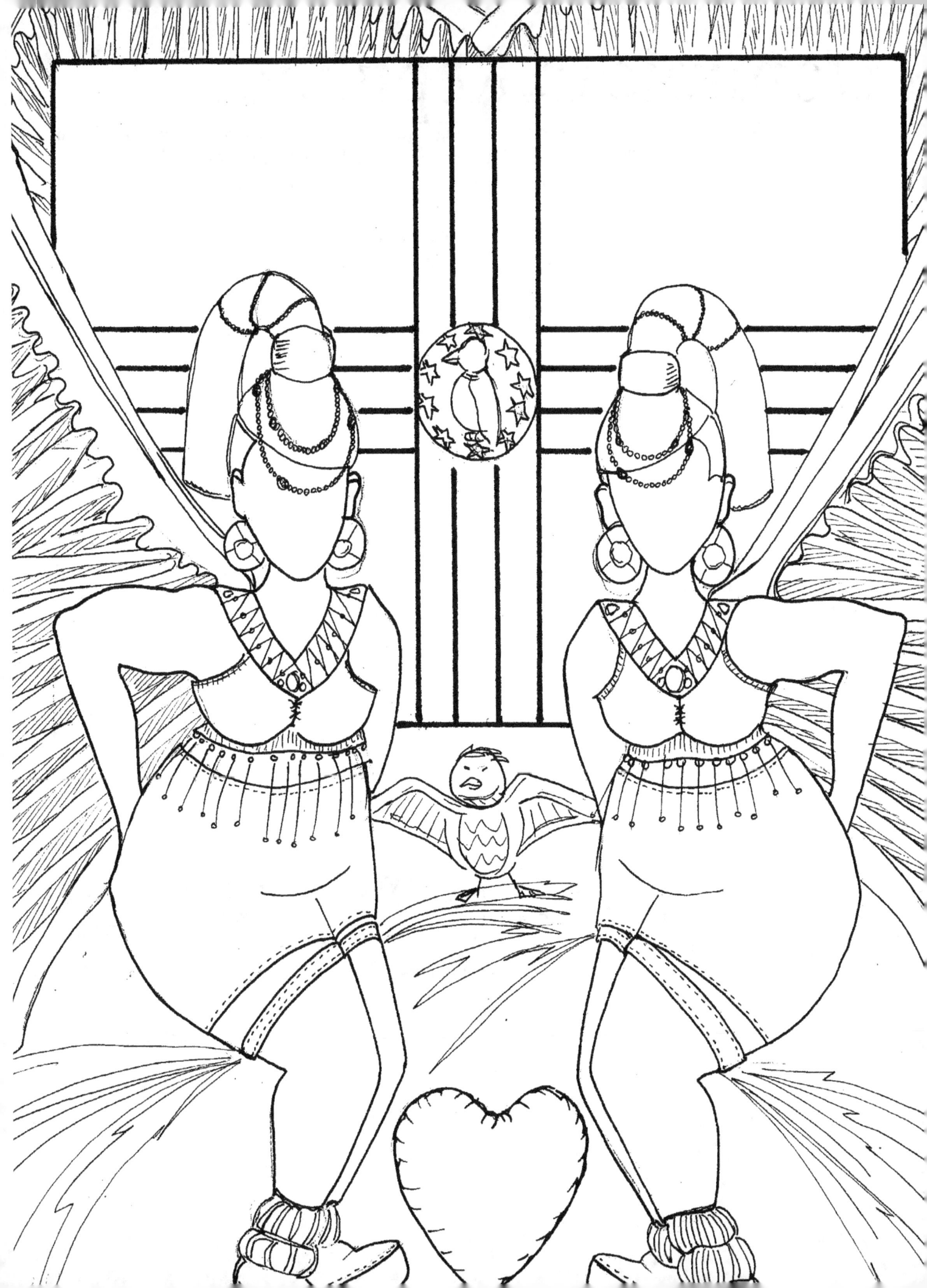

# Dominican Republic

Although the Dominican Republic is a Spanish speaking land, the people have a rich heritage shared with Haiti. Did you know that just like Puerto Rico, Haiti, and other Caribbean lands, DR has African ancestry? They were the first island in the Americas to receive enslaved peoples from Africa under the Spaniards.

Circle the names of countries below, where Africans were forced to leave and settle in D.R. during the Atlantic Salve Trade.

PANAMA

SENEGAL

GAMBIA

KENYA

UGANDA

HISPANOLA

EGYPT

MADAGASCAR

LONDON

NIGERIA

GREECE

URUGUAY

D.R. has been influenced by African language, religion, food and dance. Can you write a sentence about each word?

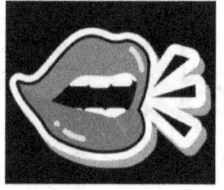 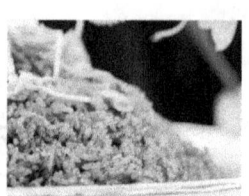 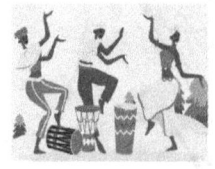

1. Language

2. Religion

3. Food

4. Dance

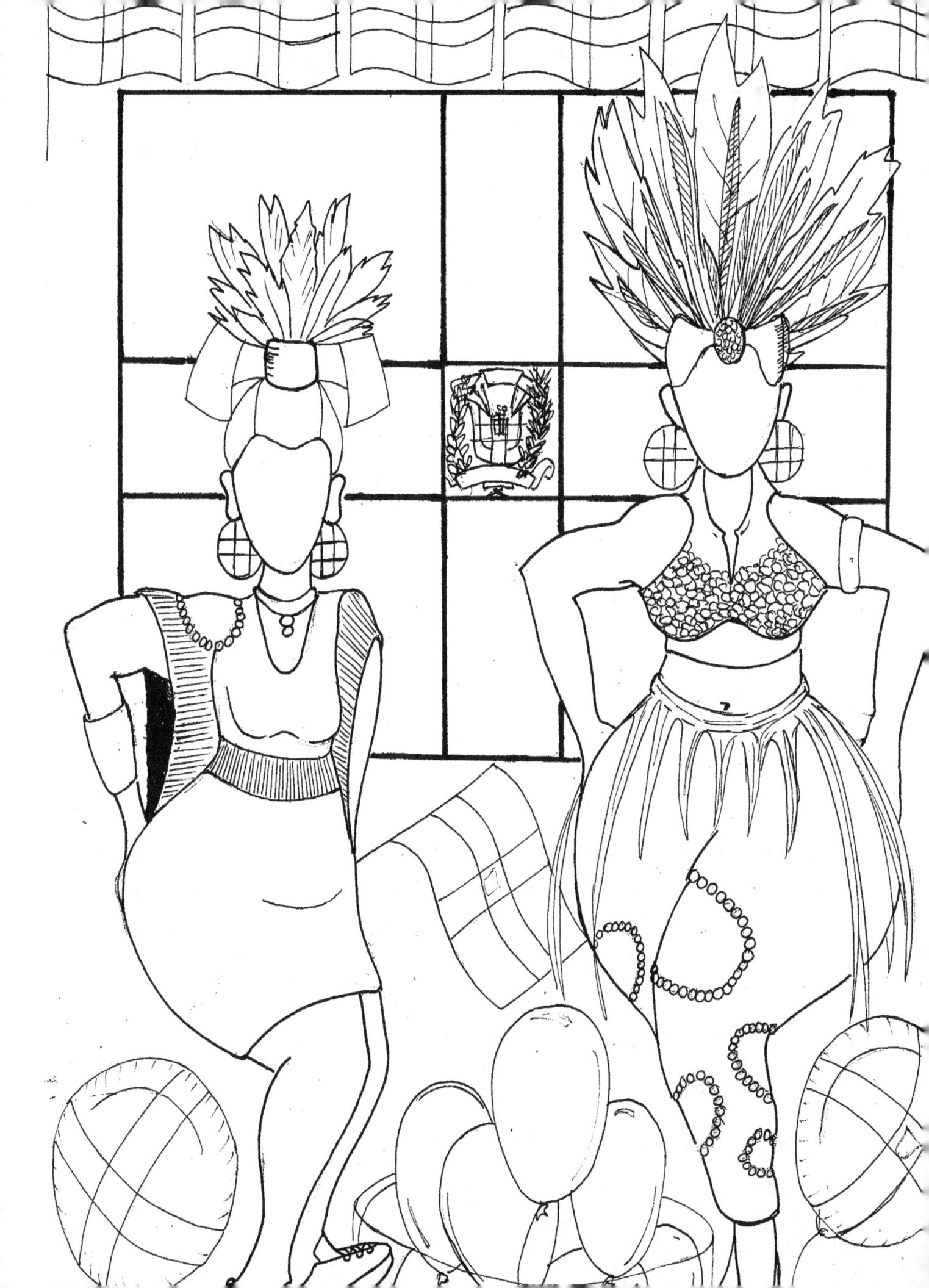

# Grenada

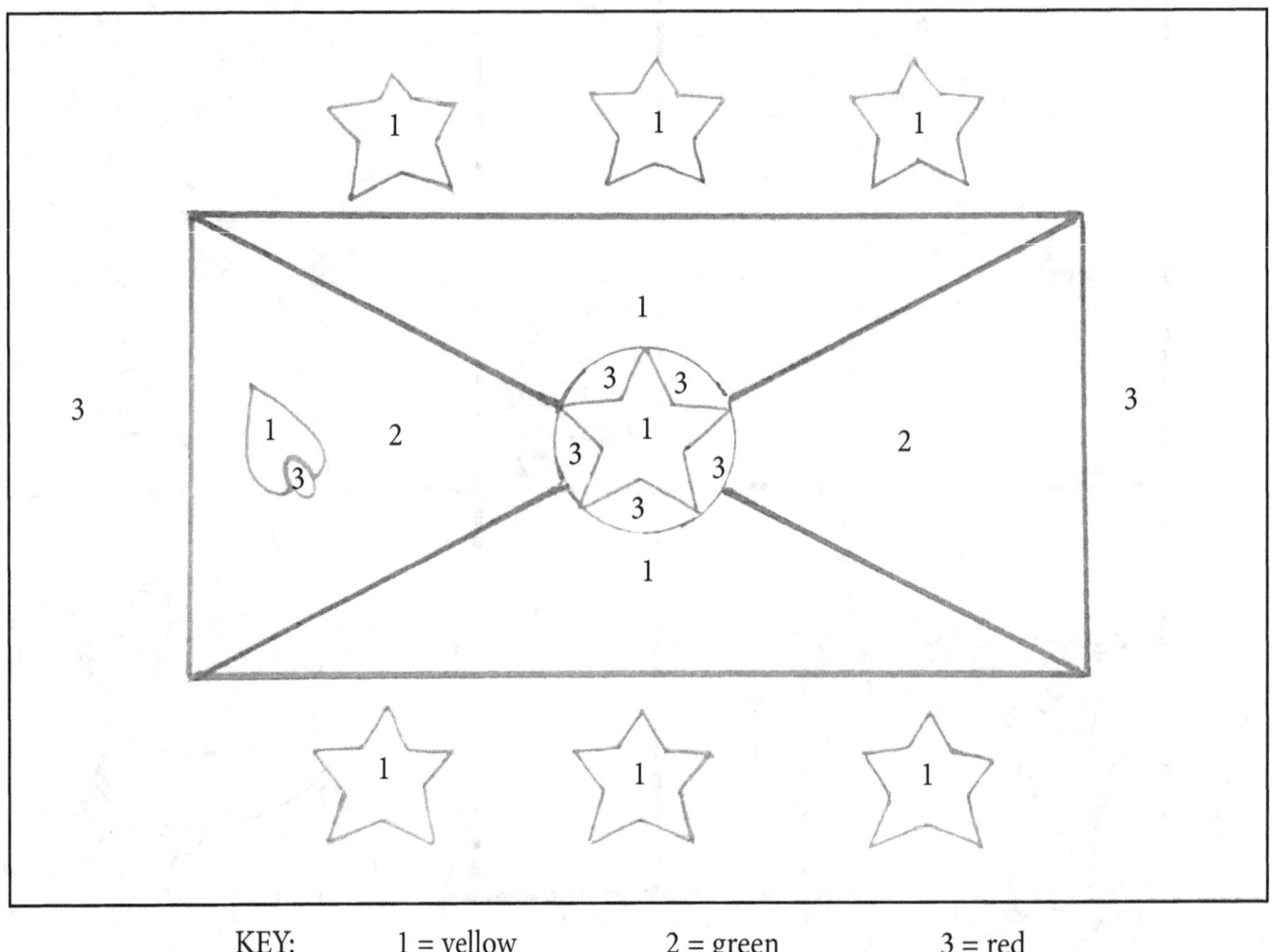

KEY:        1 = yellow        2 = green        3 = red

Uh, ohhh! There are missing objects from the flag on the next page. Use the flag above to determine (figure out) what's missing. Next, draw them directly onto the flag. Then, color!

FILL IN THE BLANK! You may need to research to get the answers to these questions.

1. _____ island is another name for Grenada.

2. Grenada has the first underwater _____ garden.

3. In the year _____ Grenada gained its independence.

4. The smaller stars in Grenada's flag represent the six_____.

5. Hurricane _____ ruined homes and other property on the island in 1994.

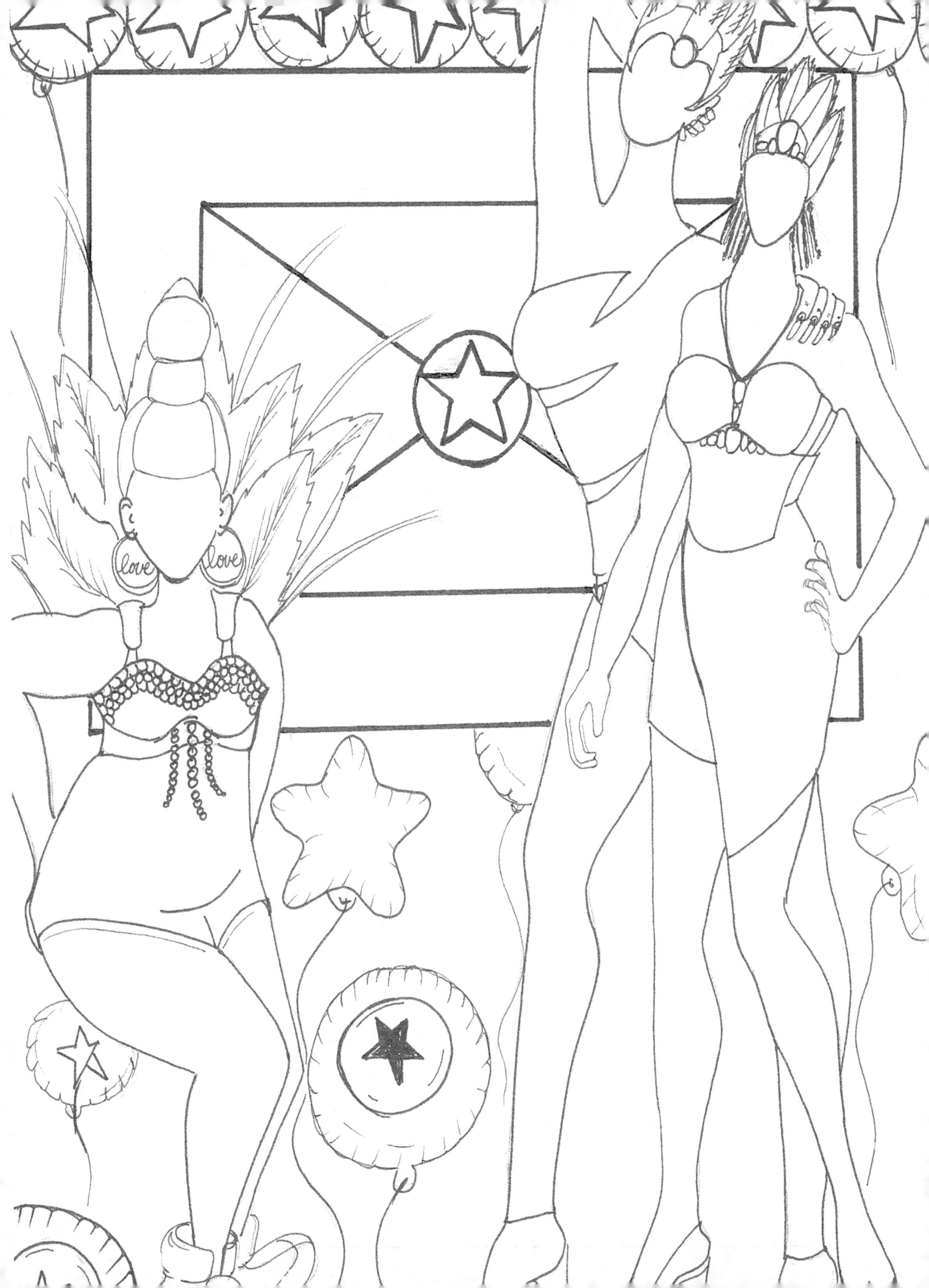

# Haiti

Did you know Haiti was the FIRST nation to
abolish the enslavement of Black peoples? After 13 years of
revolting against the French colonialists, Haiti claimed its
independence on January 1st in 1804.

If you were a Hollywood movie director, what would one of the battle scenes look like? Draw your depiction of
Haitan warriors overthrowing the French plantation owners. Use the space below as your storyboard. (Ask your
parents to help you research the battles.)

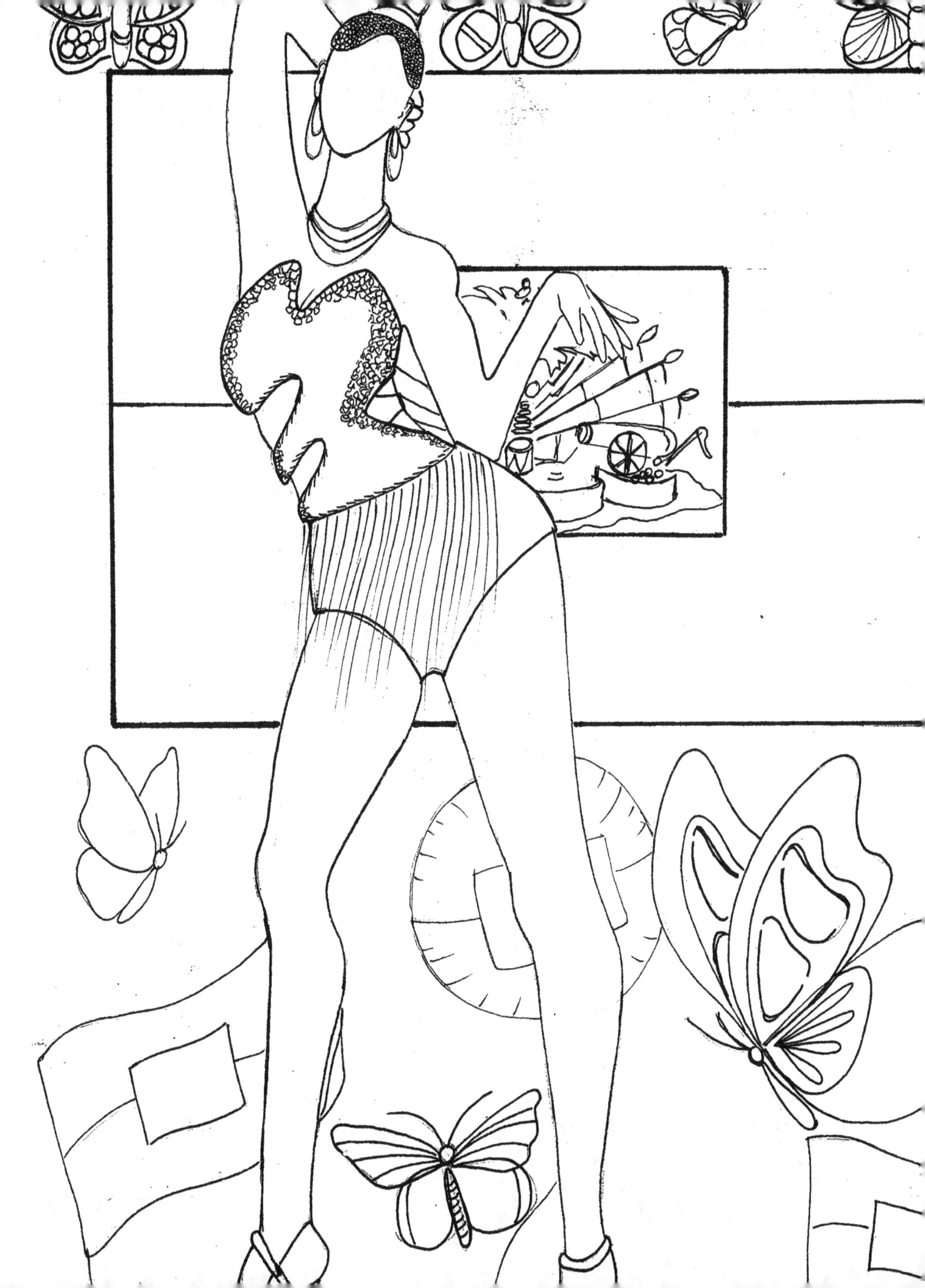

# Jamaica    WORD SEARCH

(Directions: Circle each word you find from the list in the scrambled letters below. Some words are displayed backwards, diagonal, and upwards.)

1. Caribbean

2. oxtail

3. countryside

4. jerk (seasoning)

5. reggae

6. goat

7. waterfalls

8. curry

9. patois

10. mango

```
D C P V E C S B P H S Z A W J
D Z P I L W U L Q I Z F E A N
G L J V K C O R O Q K F B T A
A A T C O U N T R Y S I D E E
E A G G E R A M E Y K Z Q R B
G C D C Q P D T X H W P C F B
V O U G O V A S Z H V J V A I
Y G L D U O C Y A L V F J L R
Y N W I G E F I L O N E B L A
D A E X A H Z L Z T R F W S C
F M T A B T A N Q K Z S O D F
Y H Q O J A X F Z S F H X U S
R M P E Y E J O J O M P P L I
P T Z X R B V V D T C K P J C
S F O A L A E N W P Y I P X G
```

EXTRAS

1. wig

2. lone

3. lip

4.. tab

5. tan

6. lot

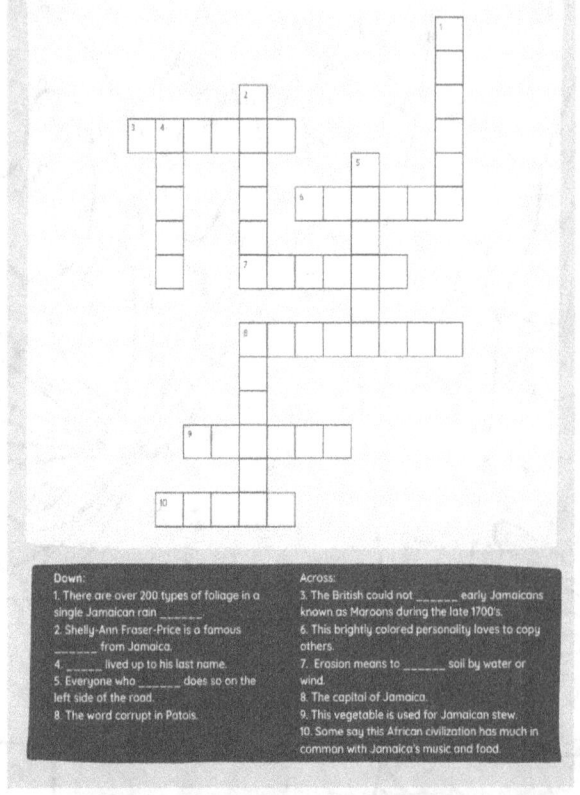

Down:
1. There are over 200 types of foliage in a single Jamaican rain _____.
2. Shelly-Ann Fraser-Price is a famous _____ from Jamaica.
4. _____ lived up to his last name.
5. Everyone who _____ does so on the left side of the road.
8. The word corrupt in Patois.

Across:
3. The British could not _____ early Jamaicans known as Maroons during the late 1700's.
6. This brightly colored personality loves to copy others.
7. Erosion means to _____ soil by water or wind.
8. The capital of Jamaica.
9. This vegetable is used for Jamaican stew.
10. Some say this African civilization has much in common with Jamaica's music and food.

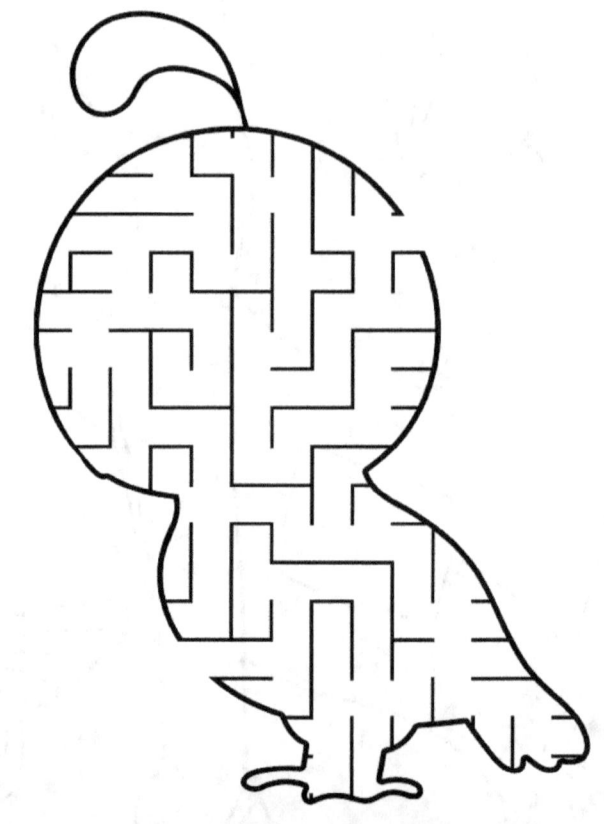

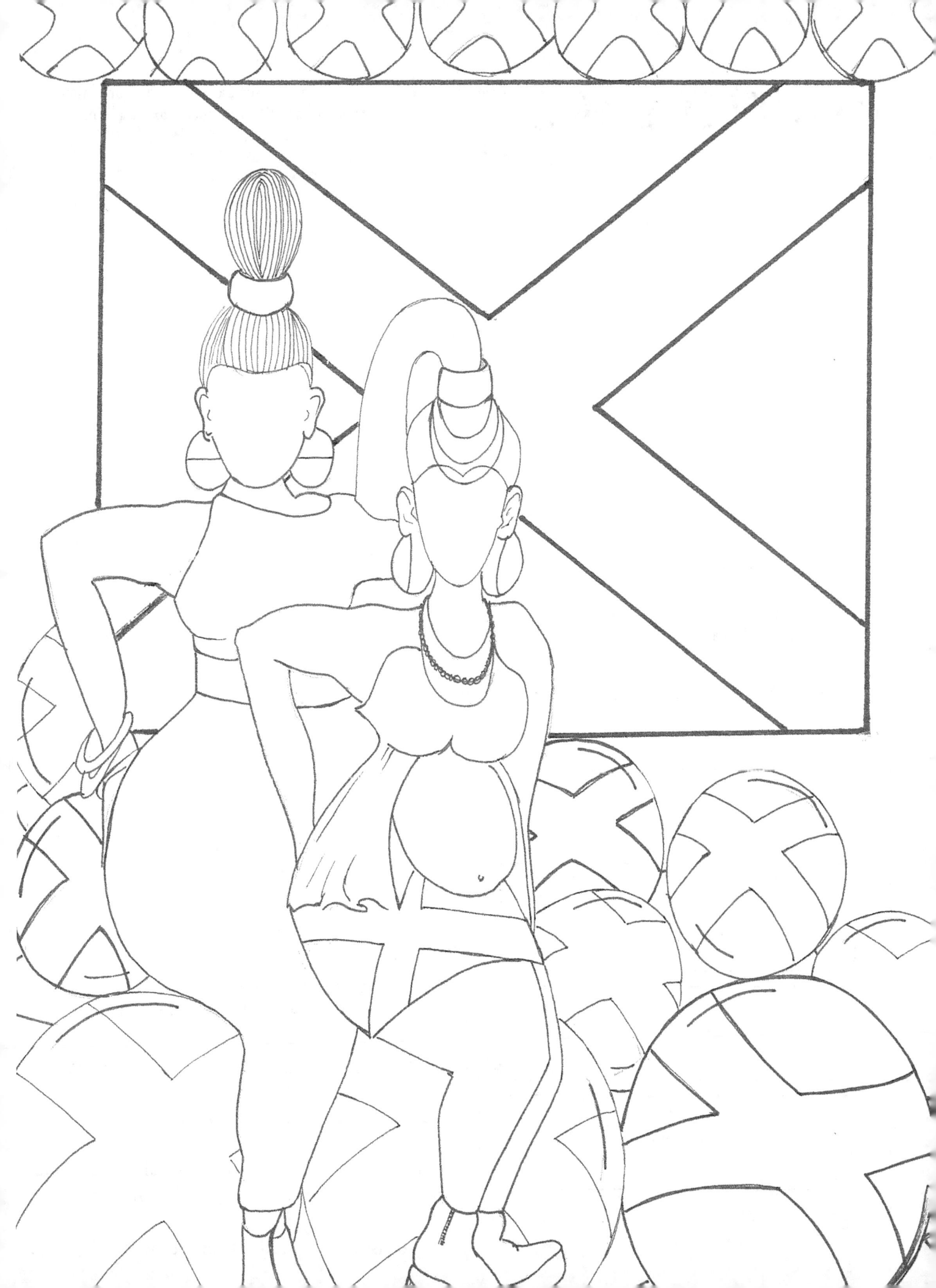

# Puerto Rico

## QUICK--QUIZ

Name the first native musica of Puerto Rico?

A.
    Jazz

B
    Plena

C
    Bomba

D
    Reggaeton

FILL IN THE BLANK.

1. Although Puerto Ricans are American, they cannot _____ for the president of the United States.

2. The largest _____ center belongs to Puerto Rico.

3. Puerto Rico is not a state, it is called a _____.

4. The people of Puerto Rico are often ccalled mestizo for having Taino, European and _____ ancestry.

5. Many consider Puerto Rico to be the oldest _____

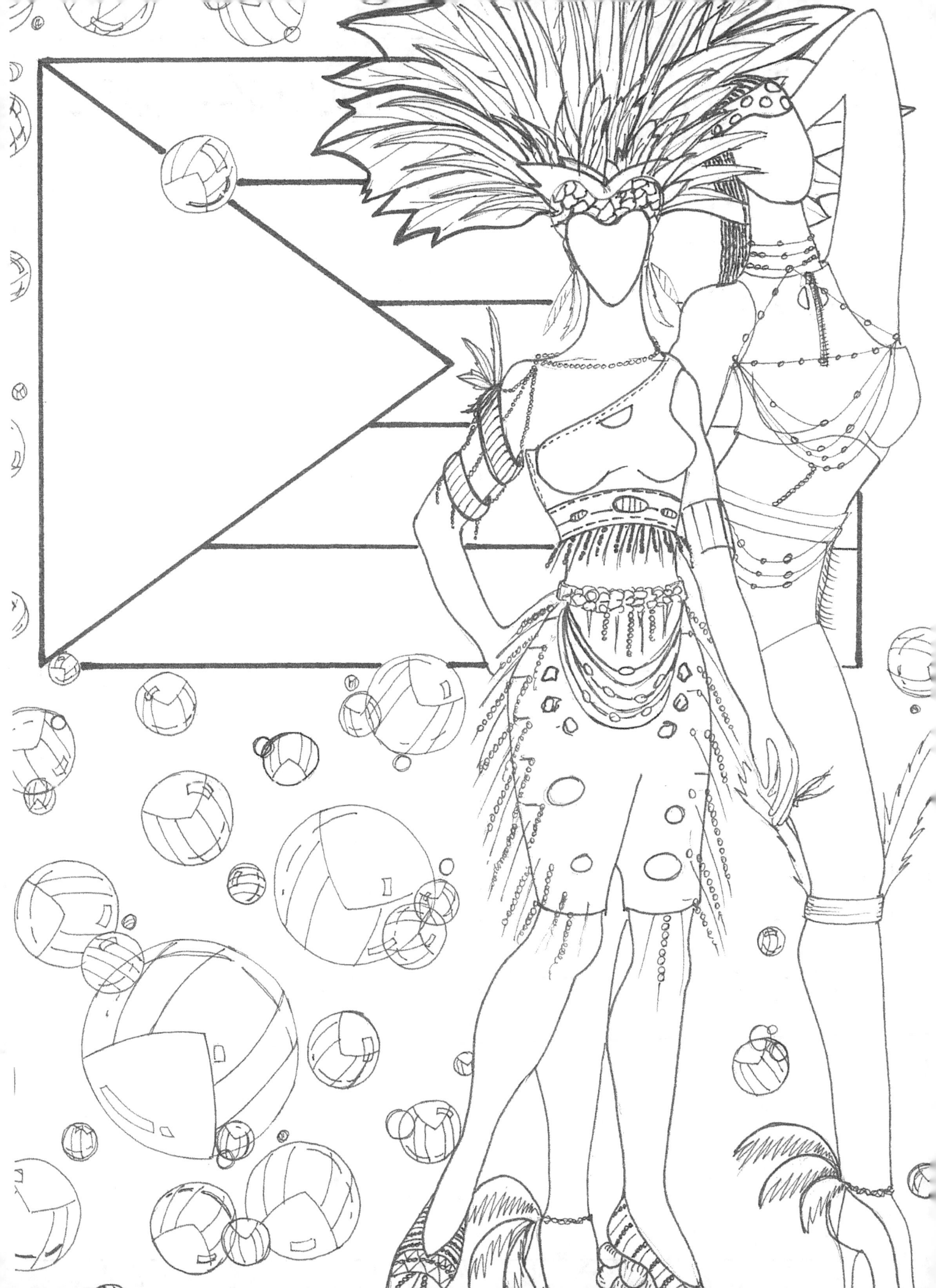

# St. Kitts & Nevis

## QUICK--QUIZ

Each year, people _____ from St. Kitts to Nevis in a special event.

A.
    fly

B.
    run

C.
    walk

D.
    swim

## QUICK--QUIZ

St. Kitts is the _____ nation of the Americas.

A.
    youngest

B.
    smallest

C.
    oldesr

D.
    biggest

Did you know....

The islands were named after Christopher Columbus? (I tell you, that man was busy!)

CAN YOU DRAW ST. KITT & NEVIS'S SEA ANIMALS UNDERWATER?

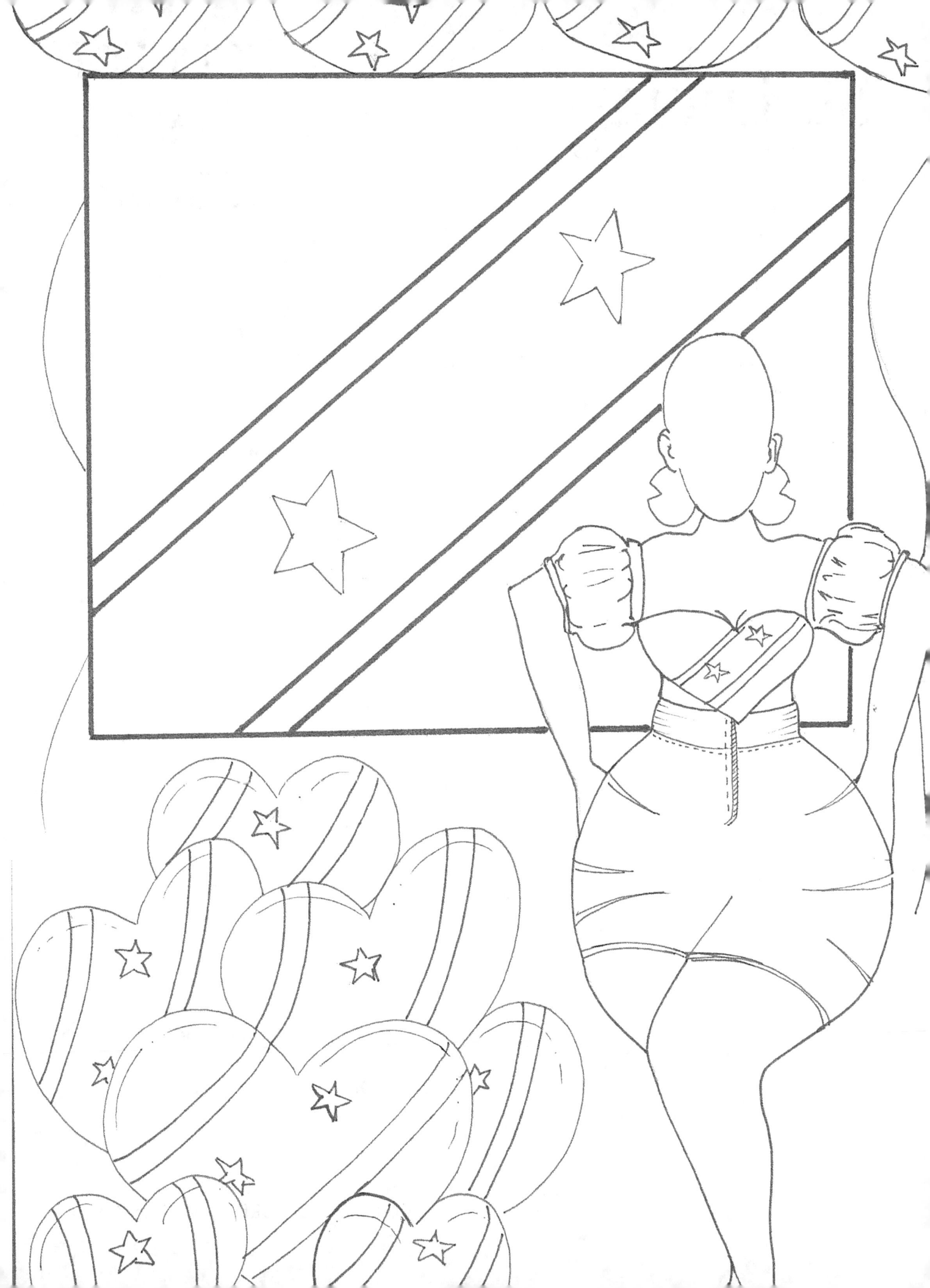

# St. Lucia

Became an independent nation in 1979

CONNECT
&
COLOR

Did you
know St.
Lucia is
named after
a woman?
It's the first
country to
do so!

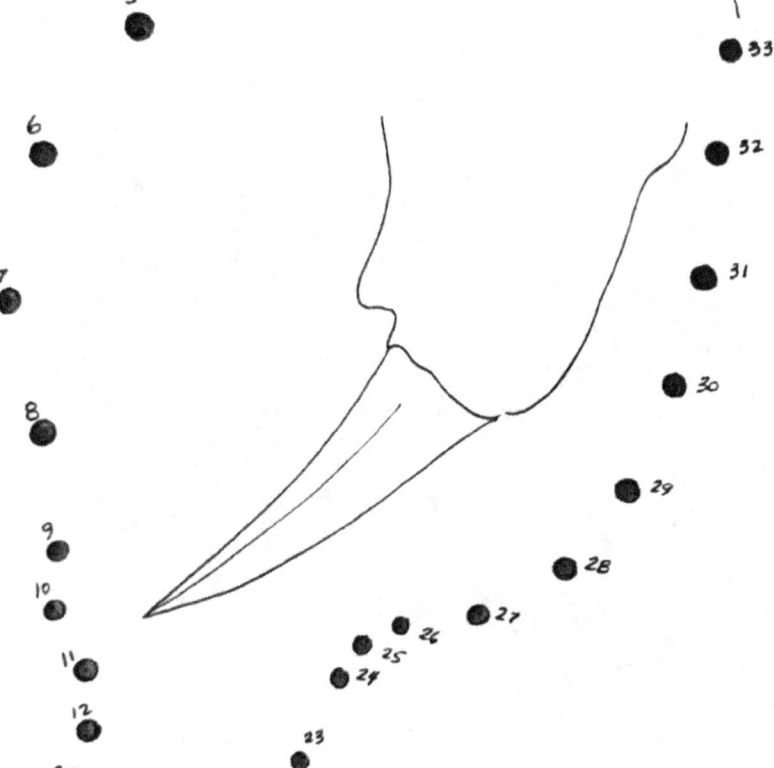

DIRECTIONS:

1. CONNECT the dots with a pen or pencil using number order
2. COLOR the bird using bright colors!

Did you know St. Lucia has a DRIVE-IN volcano? WOW!

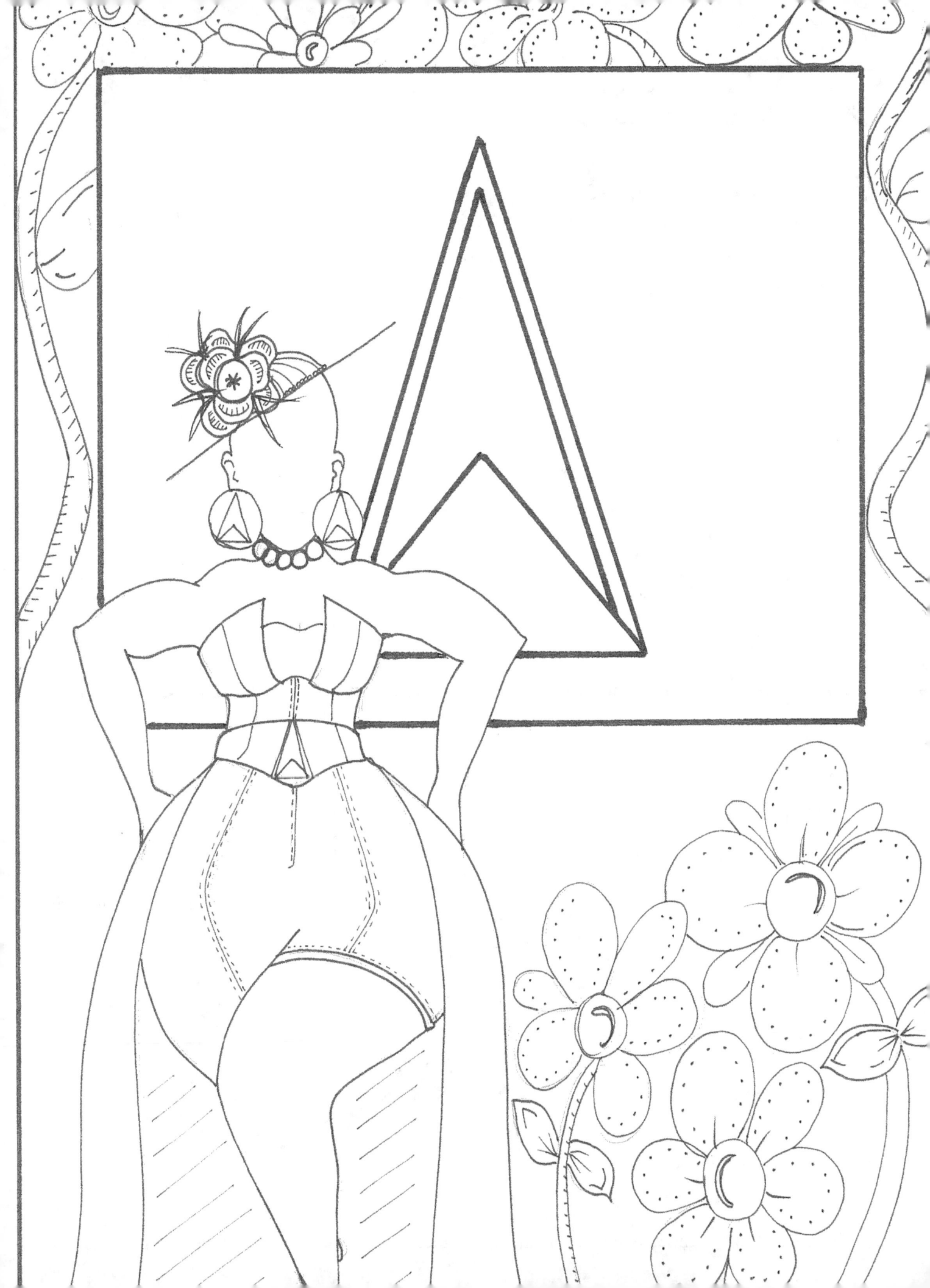

# St. Vincent & Grenadines

(Did you know St. Vincent has beaches with black sand?)

COPY THE DRAWING BELOW IN THE EMPTY GRID..
BE SURE TO START LEFT TO RIGHT.

TIC-TAC-TOE

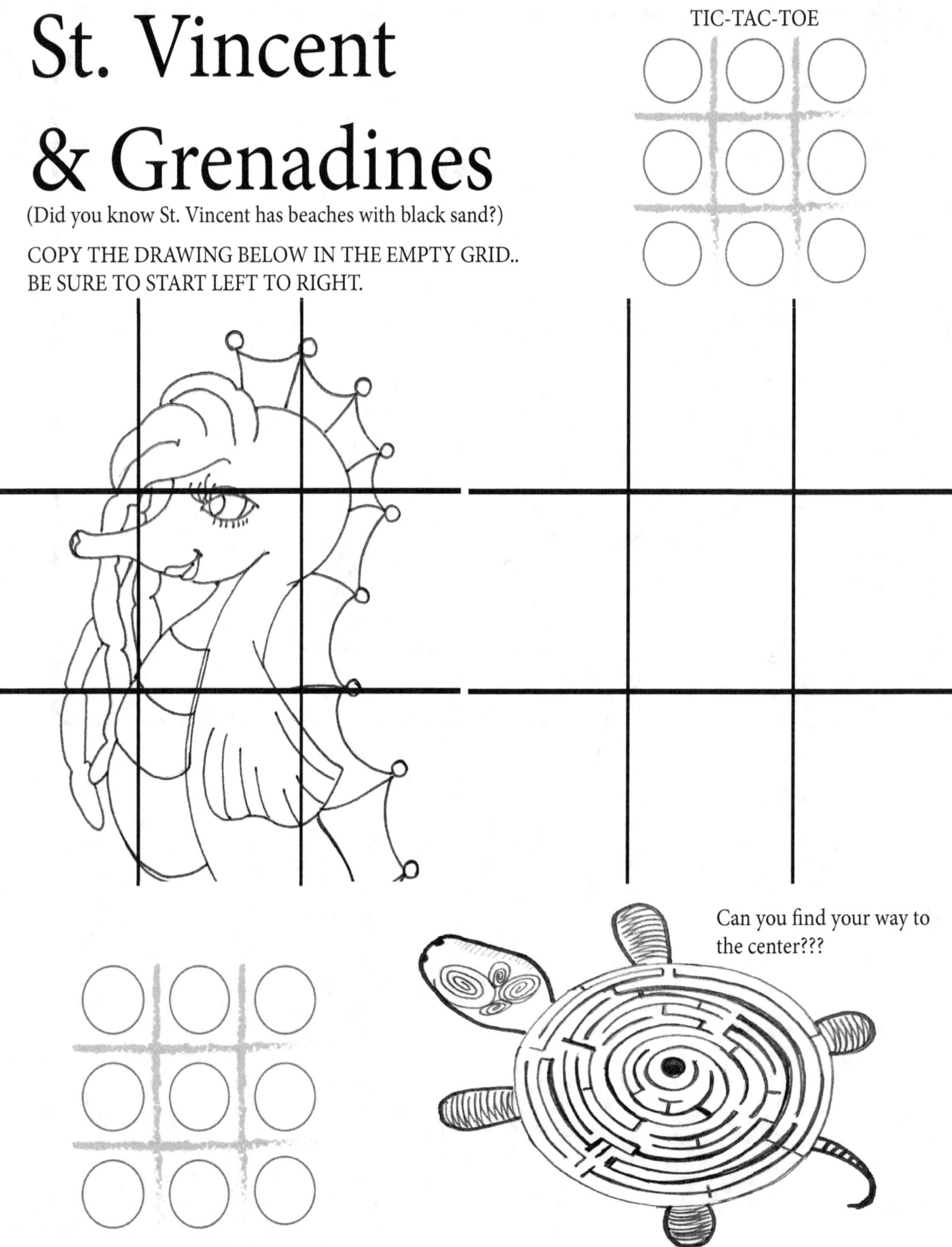

Can you find your way to the center???

Fun Fact: Only 9 of the 32 islands belonging to St. Vincent & Grenadines are occupied by humans.

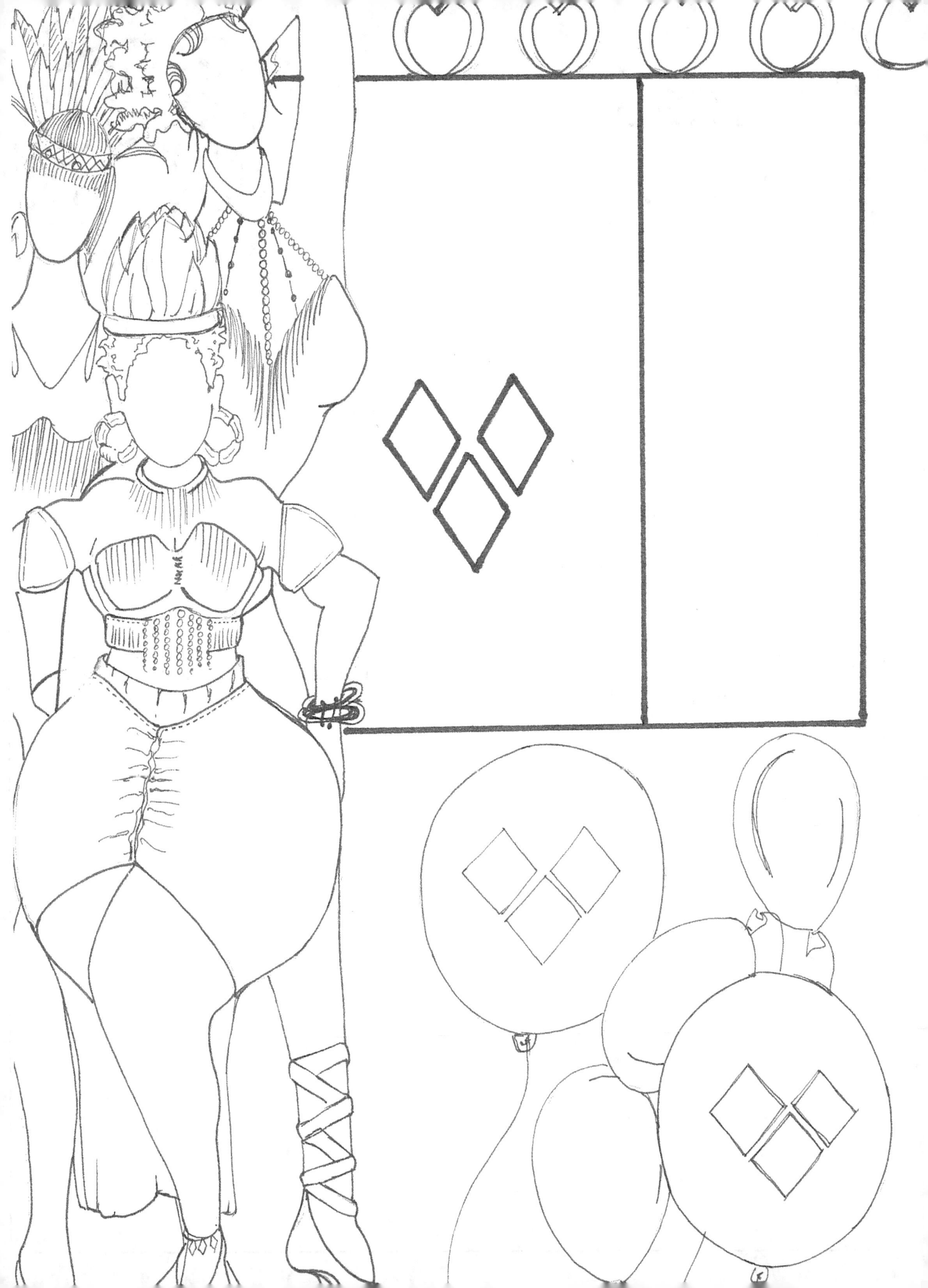

# Trinidad & Tobago

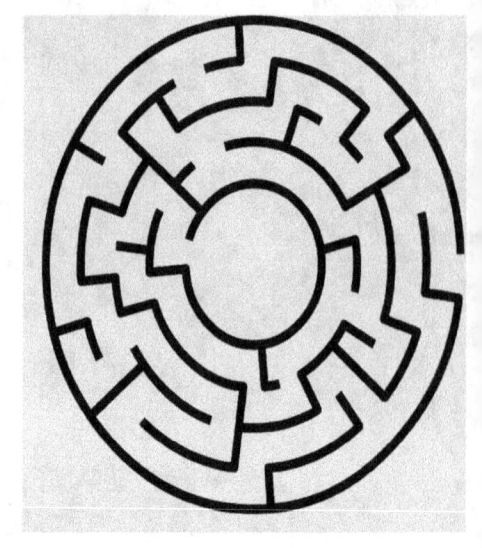

FILL IN THE BLANKS

1. The _____ drum is a musical instrument in which Trinaidad & Tobago are well-known.

2. In _____ the abolishment of slavery became a national hoilday in Trinida & Tobago. (What year?)

3. Coral reefs look more like the human _____ in Trinidad & Tobago.

4. Trinidad & Tobago are the originators of the Caribbean _____, which mimicks old French Fat Tuesdays.

5. T&T have THE hottest _____. (vegetable/seasoning.)

Uh, ohhh! Did you notice the lollipop stripes on the next page are headed in the wrong direction? Can you re-draw them in this box, correctly? Then, color!

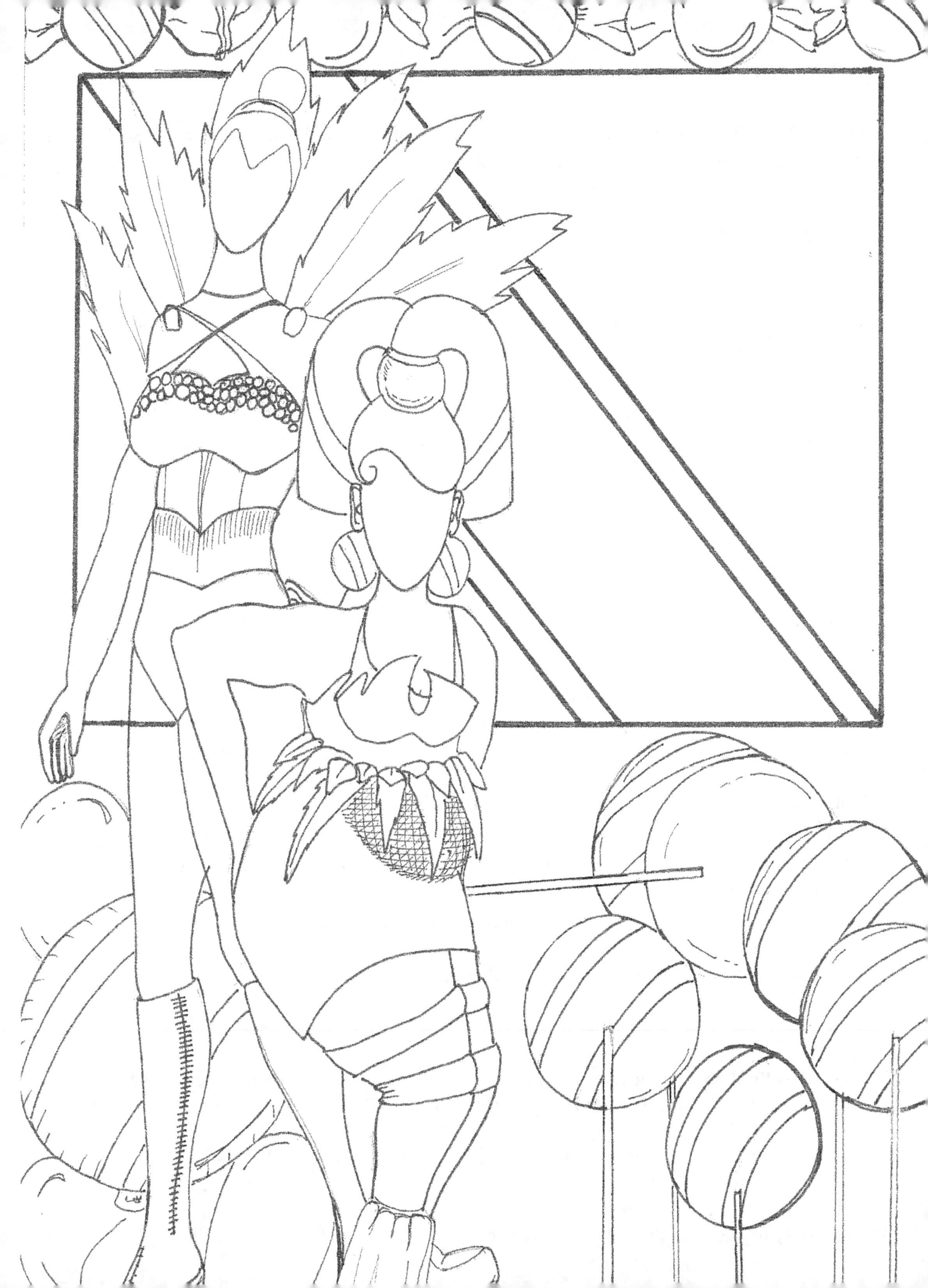

# ANSWERS

THANK YOU STOPPING BY! In an effort to be more sustainable, you will find answers to the puzzles on my website nicoleelaineavery.com I hope you're enjoying the book!

# REFERENCES

Here's where i got my information from! Maybe, you can visit these sites for more interesting facts about all fourteen Caribbean nations/territories.

1. Antigua & Barbuda- https://caribbeanwarehouse.co.uk/blog/2022/07/interesting-facts-about-antigua/ https://www.google.com/search?q=antiqua+fun+facts&oq=Antiqua&aqs=chrome.0.69i59j0i433i512j69i-57j0i131i433i512l4j0i512j0i131i433i457i512.5327j0j15&sourceid=chrome&ie=UTF-8
2. Bahamas- https://mangotreetravel.com/fun-facts-bahamas/

3. Barbados- https://www.sugarbaybarbados.com/blog/52-fun-facts-on-barbados

4. Cuba-https://www.lovecuba.com/blog/40-fun-and-interesting-facts-about-cuba/

5. Dominica- https://discoverdominica.com/en/posts/1/11-facts-about-dominica-that-will-surprise-you

6. Dominican Republic- https://www.bbc.com/travel/article/20201117-santo-domingo-the-city-that-kept-slavery-silent#:~:text=Few%20people%20realise%20that%20the,the%201490s%20by%20Christopher%20Columbus.

7. Grenada- https://www.enjoytravel.com/en/travel-news/interesting-facts/facts-about-grenada

8. Haiti- https://visithaiti.com/haiti-up-close/15-fun-facts-about-haiti/

https://www.npr.org/sections/money/2021/10/05/1042518732/-the-greatest-heist-in-history-how-haiti-was-forced-to-pay-reparations-for-freed#:~:text=Haiti%20was%20the%20first%20nation,inspire%20slave%20revolts%20back%20home.

9. Jamaica- https://www.embassyofjamaica.org/about_jamaica/history.htm

10. Puerto Rico- https://theplanetd.com/fun-facts-about-puerto-rico/

11. St. Kitts & Nevis- https://www.nothingfamiliar.com/10-things-st-kitts-and-nevis/

12. St. Lucia- https://www.google.com/search?q=fun+facts+about+st.+lucia&oq=fun+facts+about+St.+Lucia&aqs=chrome.0.0i512j0i22i30l5j0i15i22i30j0i22i30l2j0i15i22i30.15751j0j15&sourceid=chrome&ie=UTF-8

13. St. Vincent & Grenadines- https://www.enjoytravel.com/en/travel-news/interesting-facts/interesting-facts-st-vincent-and-the-grenadines

14. Trinidad & Tobago- https://iamaileen.com/trinidad-and-tobago-facts/

www.ingramcontent.com/pod-product-compliance
Lightning Source LLC
Chambersburg PA
CBHW081649220526
45468CB00009B/2600